The Love Between a Mother and Daughter Is Forever

A Blue Mountain Arts® Collection
About the Special Bond
Mothers and Daughters Share

Edited by Patricia Wayant

Blue Mountain Press™

SPS Studios, Inc., Boulder, Colorado

The Love Between
a Mother and Daughter
Is Forever

The love we share
as mother and daughter
is a bond of the strongest kind.
It is a love of the present,
interwoven with memories
of the past
and dreams of the future.
It is strengthened by
overcoming obstacles and
facing fears and challenges together.
It is having pride in each other
and knowing that our love
can withstand anything.

It is sacrifice and tears,
laughter and hugs.
It is understanding, patience,
and believing in each other.
It is wanting only the best
for each other
and wanting to help anytime
there is a need.
It is respect, a hug,
and unexpected kindness.
It is making time to be together
and knowing just what to do and say.
It is an unconditional,
forever kind of love.

— Barbara Cage

What a Mother Is
to Her Daughter...

*B*etween a mother and daughter,
there is a special love
that exists nowhere else.
A mother is someone who loves
and is never afraid to show that love.
A mother sometimes pushes aside
    her own needs
to focus on the needs of others.
A mother is a haven of love,
a listening ear when no one else cares
    or has time to listen.
A mother makes time.
A mother gives advice when asked
but always with the understanding
that it is only advice,
leaving her daughter free
to make her own choices.
Though there are some times
when mother and daughter don't agree,
a mother respects her daughter's choices,
encourages her decisions,
and listens to her reasoning.
A mother is all these things
to her daughter, and more.

— Dale Harcombe

...and a Daughter Is
to Her Mother

A daughter is a little piece
of yourself
looking back at you.
She is another chance for you
to realize the dreams
of your past.
She is a precious gift,
and adventures without end.

A daughter is your best creation.
She's a best friend
and a fashion advisor.
Only she knows why
you love purple
and hate turnips.

A daughter is never-ending love,
given and received,
and learning to love yourself.
Of all the things that
happen in a woman's life,
a daughter is the best.

— Brenda A. Morris

The Story of One Mother's Love

*M*onths before I was born,
My mother must have
Patiently waited and planned
For my arrival.

Then, at last, the day came,
And I was on the scene.
Little did she know
All that this would mean for her.

I'm sure I intruded on her privacy,
Made her nights short,
Made her food bill rise,
And drained all her energy.

Still, through all this,
She was always there
To comfort me and
Let me know she cared.

When trouble came my way,
I remember a gentle pat on the head
and her saying, with love,
"Here, can I help you with that?"

And then there were those growing pains
That come to each of us —
Too old for some things
And not old enough for others.

I would get upset and mad at the world.
Through it all, she was there
To comfort me and let me know she cared.

The teen years must have been
The worst stage to go through.
Rebellious times upset her so.
She must have shed many tears for me.

Through all this, she was
Understanding, loyal, warm,
Compassionate, loving, and caring.

We have had disagreements —
She has had her opinions and
I have had mine.
And who's to say who was right?

Although I caused her many sleepless nights,
She was always there
To comfort me and
Let me know she cared.

If there would be one thing I could ask for,
It would be that my children
Love and respect me
As I do my mother.

But even more than that,
I hope that I will
Love them as she loved me
And that I will always
Be there for them
To let them know I care.

— Judy Halderman

*B*efore she was a part of my life, I used to
dream about what it would be like to have
a daughter.
Scattered among my hopes for someone to love
and share things with were many fears of
motherhood and all its challenges.
I wondered whether I had it in me to give enough
of myself to meet the needs of a tiny new
person who would depend on me for everything.
I wondered whether I could love and care for a
beautiful daughter the way I imagined in my
dreams — completely and without reservations.
When she finally became a part of my life, I knew
right away that she was everything I had hoped
for and more.
The little fears disappeared in the rush of love I
felt, and when I held her in my arms I wanted
to stay that way forever.

— Linda Sackett-Morrison

*W*hen the nurse brought my baby in, I looked into her face and saw myself — her eyes, her skin, her expressions, her spirit. She looked up at me and smiled her first hello. A broad and mischievous grin lit up her face, a sign that told me in no uncertain terms that this was a child to be reckoned with, a child who would be worthy of great things. From that moment on my heart was all hers. I was terrified, elated, proud, and complete... all at once... On that day... we began our wonderful duet, a blend of heart, mind, and soul that continues to this day.

— Naomi Judd

Unforgettable "Firsts"

*D*ear Daughter,
the first time I held you
was a magical moment.
I remember the first time you smiled;
I still carry that memory with me.
The times I cuddled you
were cradled with tenderness.
Often and silently,
you spoke love to me with your eyes.

I wouldn't trade the countless
fingerprints you left behind
for a dozen unmarked walls.
And all the times your curiosity
led you to my closets and cupboards,
and your imagination left its mark,
only made me love you more.

I loved your giggles then,
and I love them now.
I've seen you in deep thought,
and I've seen you acting silly.
I've captured your moods and our memories
and sewn them into my heart.

When you came along,
I knew you would change my world,
but what I didn't know then
was that I could gain
a lifelong friend.

— Kathryn Leibovich

*M*other, your arms were the first to hug me;
   you could make me feel like I was
   the center of your universe
when you wrapped me up in safety,
   security,
and the warmth of belonging.
Your voice was the first to sing to me,
make me smile, and lull me to sleep.
Your hands were the first to nurture me;
you kissed away my fears and comforted me
through colds and fevers
and an endless list of childhood maladies.
Your gentle fingers smoothed my hair
   and soothed my aches and bruises.
You were the first person to encourage me,
cheer me on, give me approval,
and applaud when I did something worthy.
You are the person who taught me
what it means to be loving and loved.

— Patricia A. Teckelt

Only One Mother

*H*undreds of stars in the pretty sky,
　　Hundreds of shells on the shore together
Hundreds of birds that go singing by,
　　Hundreds of lambs in the sunny weather.

Hundreds of dewdrops to greet the dawn,
　　Hundreds of bees in the purple clover,
Hundreds of butterflies on the lawn,
　　But only one mother the wide world over.

— George Cooper

*M*ost of all the other beautiful things in life
come by twos and threes, by dozens and
hundreds. Plenty of roses, stars, sunsets, rainbows,
brothers and sisters, aunts and cousins, but only
one *mother* in the whole world.

— Kate Douglas Wiggin

The Home My Mother Built

*T*welve faded photographs,
all of me, the first few bravely
smiling, the last several hinting
at resigned endurance but
all posed in the shape of a
girl waving goodbye to
a proud mommy standing
in the hall, recording the
courage of sending her child
out to the world each August.

They are faded and bent now;
we laugh at my clothes and
Holly Hobbie lunch box
and embarrassment in
reliving those awkward gangly
years and yet, beneath
squirming blushes, there is
such wonderful sweetness
to know that the unseen heart
behind the camera that let
me loose on the world with
much prayer and love and tears
and hugs did so with the ancient
wisdom of mothers, laying down
foundations for the exuberant
joy that currents between us when,
in independent womanhood,
I come back for respite
to a world of home.

— Heidi Gwynette Lane

No Greater Gift than...
a Daughter

―∞―

*N*o one could have prepared me
   For the depth of love
That sprang into my heart for my daughter
From the very moment she was born.
She truly is a treasure,
And I will cherish her all my life.
I will brag about her and show her off
Every time I get the chance.
And though I don't know how
   it's possible,
She becomes more dear to me
With every year that passes by.
She will always be my special gift.

— Cheryl Barker

My Favorite Woman

After we've spent the day together
we talk for hours on the phone
There is always more to say

She is the only person
I can comfortably shop with
and not feel impatient
when she tries on things forever
or worry that I'm taking too long
in deciding between two dresses

Only with her can I still giggle
mostly at the silliest things
I don't offer to shorten anyone else's hems
nor tidy up anyone else's kitchen
When she borrows something
I don't ask for it back

We exchange recipes
gossip about family members
and reminisce about the past

When she criticizes, it matters
Her compliments mean more
than those of friends

She is my favorite woman to be with
I am talking about my daughter

— Natasha Josefowitz

Growing and Learning Together...

⌘

*T*hroughout the years, just watching my daughter grow from childhood to adulthood has brought me more pleasure than anyone could ever know. I have benefited so much from being her mother, and I have learned that life's most precious gift is the family around us.

— Linda E. Knight

*W*hat I treasure the most
  is the love that has grown
  between us.
Maybe that is because we have grown
in our own ways and in our own times
to be more receptive to what is
  really important in our lives.

— Elizabeth Hornsey Reeves

*D*ear Daughter,
    as you grew —
I grew alongside of you.

As you were made to feel
good about yourself,
I was also given a sense
    of self-worth
that I had never known.

As you felt the radiant warmth
    of unconditional love,
I was embraced by all that
reflected back from you.

As you lived,
    I learned,
and as you took strides,
I broadened my own steps,
    as well.

              — Lynn Barnhart

*T*he years hold precious memories,
    but most of all, they hold growth.
In a way, we grew up together.

             — Susan M. Pavlis

The Teen Years

She is in high school

She is in love
She speaks on the phone for hours
looks in the mirror endlessly
fixing her hair
trying on clothes
stuffing tissues in her bra

She is in love
She giggles incessantly
often making no sense at all
not doing her homework
eating junk food
smoking in secret

She is in love
She puts on too much makeup
had her ears pierced
goes to too many parties
and generally behaves
in ways I would consider crazy
were she not in high school

were she not in love

— Natasha Josefowitz

There were times when we struggled.
She was longing for her own independence
and searching for her own place in the world.
I remember those times as I tried to
hold her close and hold on tight to my little girl,
knowing all the time in my heart it was a
part of growing up for her and for me,
a part of life we would endure
and that eventually we would become closer
than ever before.

— Deanna Beisser

So much of the mother-daughter
tension has to do with an inability
to consult, or an unwillingness of either
mothers or daughters to admit the value
of what the other has to say.

— Cokie Roberts

Through
the Tears and Laughter...

⎯⎯⎯⎯⎯⎯⎯⎯⎯⎯⎯⎯⎯ ∞ ⎯⎯⎯⎯⎯⎯⎯⎯⎯⎯⎯⎯⎯

*F*or each moment of joy a daughter experiences,
there is a silent joy shared by her mother,
along with a silent prayer
of thanks to God for the blessing
he has given her, her child.
Behind each tear shed and each hurt felt,
there is a silent tear and a silent hurt
felt deep inside a mother's heart.

— Catherine I. DiGiorgio

*E*ach different stage turned another
page in our lives. My memory recalls
them for me: birthday parties, first days
of school, holidays, laughter, fun, and even
tears. Without a sprinkle of those tears,
even a flood of them at times, we could
not have appreciated the rainbows, starlight,
love, sharing, and caring.

— Vicki Silvers

There were difficult times
in our relationship —
times when our strong wills
overshadowed the love in our hearts.
Sometimes I chose a different path
than my mother wanted me to,
yet she was always there to show me
the way back home
and to welcome me
into her comforting arms.

— Lori Glover

With every tear that she wiped from
my eyes, every word of praise, every
smile and hug, every time she listened with
compassion or offered loving advice, I became
more confident about the surest of all loves —
the kind that only a mother can give.

— Pamela Koehlinger

A good laugh is sunshine in a house.

— William Makepeace Thackeray

Always There for
Each Other

A mother's love is a special kind of love that's always there when you need it to comfort and inspire, yet lets you go your own path. A sharing heart filled with patience and forgiveness, that takes your side even when wrong. Nothing can take its place.

— Debra Colin-Cooke

*W*hen I was little
    I depended on my mother
she nursed me
when I was sick
took me to the doctor
and told me not to worry
she would always be there
to take care of me

And now that I'm grown
and my mother is old
she depends on me
to nurse her when she's sick
take her to the doctor
and tell her not to worry
I'll always be there
to take care of her

— Natasha Josefowitz

To My Mother

*Y*ou were always there
     to help me
You were always there
to guide me
You were always there
to laugh with me
You were always there
to cry with me
But most important
you were always
there to love me
And believe me
I am always
here to love you

— Susan Polis Schutz

Mothers and Daughters
Share a Special Bond of Love

The relationship between
a mother and daughter
is comprised of a very deep
understanding of and support for
each other
It is based on an enormous
amount of emotion and love
There is no other relationship
in the world
where two women are so much
like one

When I gave birth to
my beautiful daughter
I never knew what a
special relationship
a mother and daughter could have
As she got older
and started to understand more
about being a female
I felt as if I were going through
all the stages of growing up
once again

I felt a strong urge
to protect her from anything
that could possibly hurt her
but I knew that if I did
she would not be prepared
to face the real world
So I tried to
establish the right balance
by showing her and
explaining to her
what I consider to be
the most important things in life

And I have loved her every second
of her life
I have supported her at all times
and as her mother, as a person
and as a friend
I will always continue
to cherish and love
everything about her
my beautiful daughter

— Susan Polis Schutz

As Women...

*T*he bond between women is a circle...
we are together within it.

— Judy Grahn

*W*e women bear the world, and we make it.

— Olive Schreiner

*T*he real religion of the world comes
from women much more than from
men — from mothers most of all, who
carry the key of our souls in their bosoms.

— Oliver Wendell Holmes

O you young and elder daughters!
    O you mothers and you wives!
Never must you be divided,
in our ranks you move united.

— Walt Whitman

Being a woman is being positive, natural, and
not losing your instinctive, intuitive self.

— Jean Muir

Boundless

They talk about a woman's sphere
    As though it had a limit;
There's not a place on earth or in Heaven,
There's not a task to mankind given,
There's not a blessing or a woe,
There's not a whispered yes or no,
There's not a life, or death, or birth,
That has a feather's weight of worth —
    Without a woman in it.

— Author Unknown

As Friends...

As mother and daughter,
we've always been
like best friends.
We don't take each other for granted;
we don't demand that we be
anything more than who we are.
We accept the fact that sometimes
we aren't exactly the way
we wish we could be.
We have always believed
in each other,
and I think that is what
will always be
the strongest part of our relationship.
Because of who we are,
we not only appreciate, respect,
and trust each other,
we also have the opportunity
to learn how to value
each other's uniqueness.
I am forever thankful for
the loving and caring relationship
we have as mother and daughter
and as truly the best of friends.

— Laura Medley

$\mathcal{I}$'m so glad that we're different
from a lot of mothers and daughters.
We're not just family, but true friends.
We can confide in each other
no matter what the subject.
We can share laughter and good times,
discuss life's challenges,
try to help fix each other's problems,
or just be there to listen and understand.
We can count on each other
more than anyone else in the world,
knowing we will be there for each other
    under any circumstances.
The love and support we share
provides us with confidence,
courage, and strength
    whenever we need it most.
We're more than mom and daughter...
we're best friends.

— Barbara Cage

Ten Reasons Why
We Are So Alike

_B_ecause we delight in
    other women's "Bad Hair Days,"
and we blame how we look in swimsuits
on the dressing room lights;
Because we take more snack breaks
than we should
and only regret it a little;
Because we lose track of time
in fabric stores, bookstores,
and stores with cute clerks,
and there is always one more horrific dress
we can talk each other into trying on;
Because our kitchen-table talks
have only changed in subject and drink,
and we probably keep the phone company
from going broke;
Because we both agree that men
should not be the ones designing bras
and that no actually doable
exercise video exists;
Because we are more than just
mother and daughter:
we are friends.

                             — Heidi Lebauer

_O_ daughter, lovely as thy lovely mother.

                             — Horace

Reflections

*C*ome stand beside me
What do you see
When you look in the mirror?

I see
Two people
Two women
Two hearts
Two souls
But most of all
I see a reflection of you.

I see a reflection of you...
in me.

When I look at you
I see more than my mother.

To me
You are a vibrant woman
Who has faced adversity
And has always been victorious in my eyes.

I see a woman with inner strength
Fun-loving personality
And compassion for others.

I can only hope to become
The woman you are.

I am honored
To be your daughter
Friend
And a reflection of you.

— Karyn Thompson

When a Daughter
Becomes a Mother

*F*or so many years,
I couldn't even imagine
my daughter having a child!
It seemed as though
the best thing I could do for her
was to take care of her.
I know I fought her independence
    for a while,
because I enjoyed raising her so much.
I realize now, though,
that giving a daughter her independence
is the greatest show of love
    a mother can offer,
because it gives that daughter
the opportunity to realize
the joys of motherhood for herself.

My grandchildren are among my greatest joys,
and I am so proud of my daughter —
not only for having a child,
but for being a wonderful mother.
She has taught me that
the happiness she gives me now
is as great as the happiness she gave me
when she was a little girl —
it's just different...
in a very wonderful way.

— Vicki Perkins

Of all the things I've done in my life,
I know that my greatest joy
has come from being a mother.
Sharing my daughter's life with her
has been a gift beyond compare,
and I will always treasure
each memory we have made
through the years.
As I watch her experience
these very same joys of motherhood
with her own family,
I feel more pride and love
than I ever dreamed possible.
I realize even more
that she has blessed my life
in so many ways —
and the moments I have cherished most
were spent with her.

The happiest moment of my life
came the day I first held her
    in my arms
and experienced the precious gift
of motherhood.
The second happiest moment of my life
came the day I first held her child
and experienced the great joy
of being a grandmother.

— Deanne Laura Gilbert

Letting Go

*L*etting go is not easy. But when I look at my daughter now — a beautiful young woman, strong in her convictions and determined to face life on her own terms — I feel my heart swell with pride and joy....

In one simple truth: even though her hand may slip away from mine, we will hold each other in our hearts forever.

— Nancy Gilliam

*M*emories are forget-me-nots gathered along life's way pressed close to the human heart into a perennial bouquet.

— Clara Smith Reber

For My Grown-Up Daughter

*I*t seems like yesterday
I tucked you in at night,
whispering a prayer of thanks
for another day of
having you in my life.
Not so long ago,
we were putting your baby teeth
out for the tooth fairy
and reading storybooks
until you fell asleep in my arms.
It felt as though you grew overnight
into a beautiful young lady.
Today I see you reaching out to people,
showing that one person
can make a difference in this world.
And what a difference you've made!
I know my life could never have been so
full and complete without your being
such an important part of it.
I've watched the difference you've made
in the lives of others as well.
You have a very special gift
that inspires people to be
the best they can be.
I'm so proud of all that you do,
and I hope you'll never forget that
I love you with all my heart!

— Carol Was

If We Had It to Do
All Over Again...

*D*aughter, there are things I did
when you were young
that I would do differently now.
I am stronger and wiser than I was then,
and I wish we could relive those times
and give you a perfect childhood.
But in spite of my shortcomings,
and perhaps because of those difficult times,
you have become a fine, strong young woman,
and I am so proud of you.

It is so wonderful to be able
to talk to you as a friend,
and to see you radiate the love and understanding
that is the most important aspect of our relationship.
I marvel at your wisdom
and the depth of your perception.
I am thankful that I can let go,
knowing that you will stand on your own
and become more self-assured each day.

It's wonderful to know that we can now
be supportive of each other as equals.
I value your insight, and I treasure the bond we share.
I may not be able to undo the things I wish I could,
but I can be forever thankful that
the things I hold most dear — honesty, love, integrity —
are alive and well in you.

— Judy McKee Howser

*M*om, so often I forgot to thank you
    for all those nights
you stayed up to comfort me
and assure me that it was
"all a part of growing up,"
for all the times you wiped the tears
from the hurt that only you
knew how to soothe.
As a child, I didn't always realize
the importance of your untold favors,
but now that I've grown,
I have learned to fully cherish
all the heartfelt hours you devoted to me.
Although there's nothing in the world
I could give to repay you for everything
you've done for me,
there is something I can say
to let you know how important
you are to me.
These are the words
you taught me to feel and say,
and they are, simply...
"I love you."

— Laurie Radzwilowicz

These Are Our Prayers
as Mother and Daughter

—⚭—

These are our wishes, our dreams:
That we may always be more than
close; that nothing will come
between the bond of love we share.
That I will always be there for you,
as you will be for me.
That we will listen with love.
That we will share truths and
tenderness.
That we will trust and talk things out.
That we will understand.

That wherever you go, you will be
in my heart,
and your hand will be
in my hand.

— Laurel Atherton

Dear God,
I am a daughter,
slowly moving beyond my daily needs
where I expect and accept all that is done for me.
Help me to know that one day I may be a mother, too;
not only to my own children
but to my mother,
as her needs grow greater than mine.
My mother has taught me loving and giving.
Let me never forget.

— Madeleine L'Engle

Lord, help me to be a mother,
a mother who is kind and gentle,
a mother who is firm and strong,
a mother who loves to say yes,
but who loves enough to say no.
Let my trust in you permeate
every moment of my life,
so my daughter may see and feel
and live in that trust. So it is her trust, too.

— Madeleine L'Engle

A Mother's Wishes
for Her Daughter

------------------------------ ∞ ------------------------------

I want my daughters to be beautiful, accomplished, and good. To be admired, loved, and respected. To have a happy youth, to be well and wisely married, and to lead useful, pleasant lives, with as little care and sorrow to try them as God sees fit to send. To be loved and chosen by a good man is the best and sweetest thing which can happen to a woman, and I sincerely hope my girls may know this beautiful experience. It is natural to think of it... right to hope and wait for it, and wise to prepare for it, so that when the happy time comes, you may feel ready for the duties and worthy of the joy. My dear girls, I am ambitious for you, but not to have you make a dash in the world, marry rich men merely because they are rich, or have splendid houses, which are not homes because love is wanting. Money is a needful and precious thing, and when well used, a noble thing, but I never want you to think it is the first or only prize to strive for. I'd rather see you poor men's wives, if you were happy, beloved, contented, than queens on thrones, without self-respect and peace.

— Louisa May Alcott

A mother wishes
for her daughter to always see
the goodness in this world,
to do her part in helping those
less fortunate,
to walk hand in hand with those
of less talent,
to follow those of more knowledge,
to be an equal with those
who are different;
to find her special purpose
in this world so full of choices
and to help lead those who stray;
to become her own individual —
to set herself apart from
those who are the same.

A mother wishes for her daughter
the self-confidence to say no when it is necessary
and the strength to stand alone;
to love and respect everything
that she is and will become;
to reap the fruits of her talents,
to walk with pride down the road of life,
to be humble in her successes,
and to share in the praises and joy
of others.
But most of all, a mother wishes
for her daughter to be happy.
For when she is happy,
she has the key that will open all
of the world's doors to her.

— Jackie Olson

A Daughter's Loving Tribute to Her Mother

*B*ecause of you
A daughter was born.
A life was blessed.
A thousand hugs were given.

Because of you
A little girl grew and so did her love. Happiness filtered in through every window of her home. Hopes and wishes didn't need to be realized; just being that mother's daughter was a dream come true in the girl's eyes.

Because of you
A hand was always held, whether close or far apart. A parent's loving example showed the way. Understanding was the comforter, all tucked in and warm. The girl felt sheltered from every storm.

Because of you
A teenager grew and seasons changed into other special seasons. An awkward duckling tried her best to turn into a swan. It was a time when uncertainty needed certain things — and always her role model was there, doing her best to bring in the sunlight of each new day.

Because of you
The daughter knew she would make it. She remembered all the wisdom. Inside her heart lived more beautiful memories than there were flowers in the fields. The more time passed, the more she came to realize — that she had been blessed with the most wonderful prize in the world: the complete sweetness... of love.

Because of you
A daughter was given a gift that has brought so much joy to her life. The sweet and wondrous gift... of a mother's love.

— Laurel Atherton

Mothers and Daughters

We're daughters and mothers
Not so long ago.
We give and take
And take and give
Along time's endless row.
Love is passed
And love received
To be passed on again:
A precious heirloom
Twice, twice blessed,
A spiritual cardigan.

I'll put it on
And treasure it,
The me I have received,
And when the roles
Reverse again,
I'll have what I most need.

So may our love
Go on and on,
A hundred thousand years;
Mothers and daughters,
Daughters and mothers,
Through joys and other tears.

— theholidayspot.com

The Love Between
a Mother & Daughter...

*I*t is the sweetest love of all.
It's filled with joy and serenity
and all the things that any family
could ever hope to share. It's in a
simple kiss, in a hug, or a voice
on the phone. It keeps them close
together and travels far beyond
the home.

The love between a mother and
daughter exists in a special place
...where "always" always lasts
and "forever" never goes away.

— Laurel Atherton

ACKNOWLEDGMENTS

We gratefully acknowledge the permission granted by the following authors, publishers, and authors' representatives to reprint poems or excerpts from their publications.

Judy Halderman for "The Story of One Mother's Love." Copyright © 2002 by Judy Halderman. All rights reserved.

Villard Books, a division of Random House, Inc., for "When the nurse brought..." from LOVE CAN BUILD A BRIDGE by Naomi Judd. Copyright © 1993 by Naomi Judd. All rights reserved.

Heidi Gwynette Lane for "The Home My Mother Built." Copyright © 2002 by Heidi Gwynette Lane.

Natasha Josefowitz for "My Favorite Woman," "She is in high school...," and "When I was little...." Copyright © 2002 by Natasha Josefowitz. All rights reserved.

William Morrow and Company, a division of HarperCollins Publishers, Inc., for "So much of the mother-daughter..." from WE ARE OUR MOTHERS' DAUGHTERS by Cokie Roberts. Copyright © 1998 by Cokie Roberts. All rights reserved.

Debra Colin-Cooke for "A mother's love is...." Copyright © 2002 by Debra Colin-Cooke. All rights reserved.

The Crossing Press for "The bond between women... " from THE WORK OF A COMMON WOMAN by Judy Grahn. Copyright © 1978 by Judy Grahn. All rights reserved.

André Deutsch for "Being a woman is..." by Jean Muir from SO MUCH WISDOM, edited by Christina Foyle. Copyright © 1984 by Christina Foyle. All rights reserved.

Laura Medley for "As mother and daughter...." Copyright © 2002 by Laura Medley. All rights reserved.

Heidi Lebauer for "Ten Reasons Why We Are So Alike." Copyright © 2002 by Heidi Lebauer.

Karen Thompson for "Reflections." Copyright © 2002 by Karen Thompson. All rights reserved.

Harold Shaw Publishers for "Dear God... " and "Lord, help me to be a mother..." from MOTHERS & DAUGHTERS by Madeleine L'Engle. Copyright © 1997 by Crosswicks, Ltd. All rights reserved.

theholidayspot.com for "Mothers and Daughters." Copyright © 2002 by theholidayspot.com. All rights reserved.

A careful effort has been made to trace the ownership of selections used in this anthology in order to obtain permission to reprint copyrighted material and give proper credit to the copyright owners. If any error or omission has occurred, it is completely inadvertent, and we would like to make corrections in future editions provided that written notification is made to the publisher:

SPS STUDIOS, INC., P.O. Box 4549, Boulder, Colorado 80306.